RUNNING A CLEAN RACE
A GUIDELINE FOR SEXUAL PURITY IN MINISTRY

Dr. Steven A. Jirgal

Published by The Core Media Group, Inc., P.O. Box 2037, Indian
Trail, NC 28079.

Printed in the United States of America.

RUNNING A CLEAN RACE

When examining the root causes of justifiable dismissal of a minister, you'll find that they fall into one or more of the following categories:

A. Self: when the ministry becomes "All about me."
B. Silver: when money becomes the object of pursuit.
C. Sloth: when the minister becomes lazy and puts the calling on "Auto pilot."
D. Sex: when inappropriate sexual behavior is an acceptable part of his lifestyle.

When one or more of these attitudes or behaviors arise in a minister's life, not only is the ministry over for the individual, but a scar is left behind that may never disappear.

The purpose of this project is to alert those in ministry to the possibility, dangers of, and consequences of sexual temptation and sin. It is targeted to the men in ministry although sexual failure can ensnare the women who are involved in ministry as well.

In Hebrews 12:1, we read, "Therefore, since we have so great a cloud of witnesses surrounding us, let us also lay aside every encumbrance and the sin which so easily entangles us, and let us run with endurance the race that is set before us…"

Here we see a differentiation between two problems for the Christian. There are things in our lives that are encumbrances. These things are not necessarily sin, but they can get in the way of us ministering effectively. Taking on too many responsibilities, not resting enough, exercising too much or not enough are not sins in and of themselves, but they all carry with them the possibility of hindering our ministry and we are instructed to lay them aside.

Then the writer says we are also to lay aside "The sin that so easily entangles us." This seems to indicate that for all of us there is a particular sin that can trip us up and prevent us from running effectively. For many men *The sin* may be one that is sexual in nature.

A REALITY CHECK

The Bible tells us that Solomon was the wisest man in the world. We also know that besides Jesus, David, *A man's after God's own heart*, can be labeled the holiest man in the world. Scripture also reveals that physically, Sampson was the strongest man in the world. Besides being followers of Jehovah, what do these men have in common? The answer is each of them had fallen sexually.

This answer is followed by a question: If the wisest man, the holiest man, and the strongest man could not control their passions, why do ministers think that they are strong enough, wise enough, and holy enough to control theirs? The key is to find out why ministers fall and to build safeguards against falling themselves.

THE BREADTH OF THE PROBLEM

Years ago, Dr. Howard Hendricks talked about being in a seminary class at Dallas Theological Seminary. Before the group of men, the professor stood up and said, "Men don't think that for 10 minutes of rolling in the sheets, you can't sacrifice everything you hold dear."

The tragedy of that scenario was that a short time after that, one of those men did in fact, fall into sexual sin. The ultimate tragedy of that scenario was the fact that it was the professor who fell.

What is it that causes men of God to fall into sexual temptation and sexual sin? Is it as prevalent as we think or is it something we don't need to deal with?

FALLING BY THE NUMBERS

"A number of years ago, a national conference for church youth directors was held at a major hotel in a Midwestern city. Youth Pastors by the hundreds flooded into that hotel and took nearly every room. At the conclusion of the conference the hotel manager told the conference administrator that the number of guests who tuned into the adult movie channel broke the previous record. It far and away out-did any other convention in the history of the hotel."[1]

To be sure, men do fall into sexual temptation and sin. And to be absolutely sure, many of those who fall are men who were involved in vital ministry.

Not long ago, Dr. Howard Hendricks identified 246 men who were involved in full-time ministry who experienced moral failure within two years of each other. Each of these men would have confessed to being committed followers of Christ.[2] Many would believe that it is impossible. They doubt that members of the clergy could be involved in such a way. How is it possible that men could preach in the pulpit on Sunday and then be involved in an illicit affair later in the week?

The results of a leadership magazine surveyed 300 pastors who responded to their survey. Twenty-three percent had indicated that they had done something sexual with someone other than their spouse. Twelve percent reported having sexual intercourse with someone other than their spouse. Sixty-one percent admitted to fantasizing occasionally about having sex with someone other than their spouse. Twenty-five percent indicated that they sexually fantasize weekly or even daily.[3]

Though these statistics are hard to believe, they are reality. The sooner those involved in ministry realized that people in ministry fall just like people who are not in ministry, the sooner we will be able to turn the tide on those involved in ministry plunging morally.

THE ROOT OF THE PROBLEM

Here is the bottom line: For men, sexual temptation has an incredibly strong pull. Many women may not understand this...they have their own areas of struggle. But for men this sexual pull is both physical as well and mental. And moral failure will run the gamut from pornography to rape—even among those called into the ministry.

The problem of men falling lies in the fact that sexuality for men is such a strong drawing point. A man's sexuality is very important to him, and he is driven sexually. In this way, men are vastly different from women. "Men do think about sex more than women. They think about it, dream about it, and daydream about it more than many people realize. For several times an hour to several times a day, a sexual thought bombards the male mind depending of course on the individual man. Many typical male characteristics find their expression through sex. The male performance drive finds an outlet in the sexual relationship. Men want to perform well sexually."[4]

"The main difference between men and women in this area is that women want intimacy, communication, and relationships in the context of security and family. Men however are driven to excessive behavior. This drive is focused primarily on sex, power, and money probably in that order. Power over people and circumstances in their lives, their wives, and their children are all expressed in this drive."[5] You will not find many people who will disagree about the importance of sexuality in a man's life. However, what is the cause for letting the fire escape the fireplace?

THE SLIPPERY SLOPE

How do men allow sexual temptation and immorality to become part of their lives? The answer is that it happens gradually. A man doesn't go from his wedding day where he stands in front of a church, his friends, his family, his wife, and a minister and make promises to love her and keep himself to her 'till death do they part one day, then the next day, find sexual fulfillment in another partner. That is not normal, that is not natural, and that is not what you would expect.

However, men do slide into sexual temptation and sexual sin gradually. Oftentimes, it starts with the use of pornography. Many years ago, exposure to pornography was more difficult. Pornography was limited primarily to magazines and adult movie theatres. But today, with the technology that has developed, pornography can come right into your home. It doesn't have to be delivered through the mail or picked up at a store. A person doesn't have to drive over to an x-rated movie theatre. Simply by pushing a button, anything pornographic from dialogue to videos can appear on the computer screen. So, a man in the privacy of his home or office can experience a sexual relationship through pornography without anybody noticing.

Chuck Swindoll wrote in *Growing Strong in the Seasons of Life* about this particular sexual sin, "Deterioration is never sudden. No garden suddenly over grows with thorns. No church suddenly splits. No buildings suddenly crumble. No marriage suddenly breaks down. No nation suddenly becomes a mediocre power. No person suddenly becomes base. Slowly almost imperceptibly, certain things become accepted that once were rejected. Things once considered hurtful are now secretly tolerated. At the outset, it appears harmless, perhaps even exciting. But the wedge it brings leaves a gap that grows wider as moral erosion joins hands with spiritual decay. The gap becomes a Canyon. The way which seems right becomes in fact, the way of death. Solomon wrote that, he ought to know."[6]

GRADUATING DESIRES

Pornography and other forms of sexual baseness do not occur overnight. They slowly creep into a man's mind, whether he is a minister or not. The hard thing about sexuality is that when you dabble in sexual activity, it never is enough. At first, soft pornography may be enough to feed your desires. Then, after a period of time, that will not meet your needs. Then you have to be involved with pornography at a higher level. Sometimes that comes in the form of stronger more overt videos, sometimes it's a visit to a gentleman's club or phone sex. Although this will meet a person's need for a while, that too will graduate a person into a higher level of sexual temptation and sexual immorality. Before long, the person will have to act out on those non-contact fantasies.

"The real power of pornography is that it provides men with the ultimate fantasy fulfillment without the risk of emotional rejection that often accompanies sexual relations with real women. In normal sexual relations, our fragile male egos are on the line and often the slightest rejection of our advances from our wives can drive us quickly into seclusion, brooding, and hurt. Pornography solves the problem. Here there exists a seemingly unceasing supply of super attraction inviting women always available, always willing, and who give the impression that each reader/viewer is very special. Pornographic literature plays with our minds at the deepest levels."[7]

If this behavior goes unchecked, the natural tendency is for things to get a little more serious over a period of time. Sooner or later, because of the call to a life of ministry is to agree to live your life in a fishbowl, a person's illicit behavior will become public. Those in the media are dying for exposure. No wonder the church has lost its grip on holiness. "No wonder it is so slow to discipline its members. No wonder it is dismissed by the world as irrelevant. No wonder so many of its children reject it. No wonder it has lost its power in many places and that Islam and other false religions are making so many converts. Sensuality is easily the biggest obstacle to godliness among men today and is wreaking havoc in the church. Godliness and sensuality are mutually exclusive and those in the grasp of sensuality can never rise to godliness while it's in its sweaty grip."[8]

KEY STEPS IN RUNNING CLEANLY

How does a minister remain sexually pure? How can a man of God remain a man of God? Is it possible for a minister to run a clean race given the fact that so many have fallen? The answer is yes! There are several steps that need to be taken on the road of holiness in order for a minister to remain pure.

1 - EMBRACE THE POSSIBILITY OF FALLING

You must understand that you are not Superman, that temptation follows every man. Sexual temptation is a big dog that bites very hard and may bite often. It may be helpful to evaluate those who have fallen morally to see what they were involved in or not involved in -which led to their failure. In the study that doctor Howard Hendricks did where he evaluated 246 members of the ministry who had fallen, he found four common denominators among these men:

1. None were involved in a personal accountability group.

2. Each had ceased to invest in the daily personal time of prayer, Scripture reading and worship.

3. Over 80% of them became sexually involved with another woman as a result of counseling the woman. In other words, they were spending significant portions of their schedules with women other than their wives.

4. Without exception, each of the 246 had been convinced that moral failure "will never happen to me."[9]

Keeping safe involves realizing that if it could happen to 246 members of the clergy then it could happen to you as well.

2 - COUNT THE COST

Step two is to have a clear understanding of what's at stake. If a regular member of the church falls, or a member of society falls morally, the church looks at that person a certain way and may be angry, disappointed, and may voice their disapproval. But when a minister falls, it could prove tremendously more damaging to the Christian faith. When a minister falls, it gives reason for other people to fall and it does immeasurably more damage in the church and in society.

Jerry White notes, "One of my friends, Cliff, had been moving toward Christ for a number of years.

Several times he was almost ready to commit his life to Christ. He told me, 'I started going to church. Then the pastor ran off with the organist. It seemed that every time I reached the place where I trusted a Christian, they did some dumb thing like that, so I backed off.'"[10] Those Christians who this searching young man trusted sacrificed his Salvation for their pleasures. It's just not worth the cost. There is a deep cost to those around you when you fall morally, and you have to embrace that possibility.

Another area that you have to count the cost in is in your own personal life and the lives of those that are closely associated with you. If more people would keep in mind what Chuck Swindoll in *The Finishing Touch* writes perhaps this temptation wouldn't scream so loudly;

> *Following is an incomplete list of what you have in store after your immorality is found out:*
>
> *1. Your mate will experience the anguish of betrayal, shame, rejection, heartache, and loneliness. No amount of repentance will soften those blows.*
>
> *2. You and your mate can never again say that you are a model of fidelity-suspicion will rob her/him of trust.*
>
> *3. Your escapade will introduce to you and your mate's life the very real probability of a sexually transmitted*

disease.

4. The total devastation your sinful action will bring to your children is immeasurable. Their growth, innocence, trust, and healthy outlook on life will be severely and permanently damaged.

5. The heartache you will cause your parents, family, and your peers is indescribable.

6. The embarrassment of facing other Christians who once appreciated, respected, and trusted you will be overwhelming.

7. If you're engaged in the Lords work, you will suffer the immediate loss of your job and the support of those with whom you worked. The dark shadow will accompany you everywhere and forever. Forgiveness won't erase it.

8. Your fall will give others license to do the same.

9. The inner peace you enjoyed will be gone.

10. You will never be able to erase the fall from yours or other's mind. This will remain indelibly etched on your life's record regardless of your later return to your senses.

11. The name of Christ whom you once honored will be tarnished, giving the enemies of faith further reasons to sneer and jeer.[11]

So, counting the cost of a moral failure is paramount if one is going to remain clean.

3 - DEVELOP ACCOUNTABILITY

HB London Jr. is Vice President of ministry outreach and pastoral ministries at Focus on the Family. He says that one way that men can stay pure is to be surrounded. He says that one of our problems is that men live un-surrounded. They make themselves vulnerable by convincing others they are strong enough to resist temptation alone. "I can handle this by myself" they tell themselves. "I don't need anybody."[12] That's a tremendous danger and a man who has that attitude is setting himself up for failure.

As a man of God, you have to commit to a personal accountability group. Rod Handley was the chief financial officer for the fellowship of Christian athletes. Years ago, in an accountability group that he was in they developed ten questions that every accountability group ought to be asking:

1.   Have you spent daily time in the scriptures and in prayer?
2.   Have you had any flirtations or lustful atti-

tudes, tempting thoughts, or exposed your-self to any explicit materials which would not glorify God?

3. Have you been completely above reproach in your financial dealings?

4. Have you spent quality relationship time with your family and friends?

5. Have you done your 100% best in your job, school, etc?

6. Have you told any half-truths or outright lies putting yourself in a better light to those around you?

7. Have you shared the gospel with an unbe-liever this week?

8. Have you taken care of your body through daily physical exercise and proper sleeping habits?

9. Have you allowed any person or circum-stance to rob you of your joy?

10. Have you lied to us on any of your answers today?[13]

If a man would get into an accountability group where these questions were asked, it would great-ly help him to run a clean race.

So, accountability is very important. It is a time for personal prayer, scripture reading, and ques-tions that are asked by the men of the group. You cannot substitute time with God studying His Word, praying, worshiping Him, and the gathering of an accountability group. This is simply a discipline you must establish.

4 - BUILD PARAMETERS

You must look at how you council women and how much time you spend with a woman who is not your wife. Many churches do not have a policy in terms of men counseling women. In churches where I have served men did not counsel women after hours and we did not council women alone without an open door. All of our office doors contained windows allowing someone to look in. The door was kept open when a woman was present for counseling and even when meeting with a female staff member.

You must have rules in place and decide ahead of time what you will do when a particular situation arises. If you decide what you're going to do about a situation before you are in the situation, it removes emotions from the decision-making process.

Some guidelines regarding this may include:

- Sitting down with your office assistant (with the door open) and discussing what is to be expected relationally.
- Informing them that you will not take them out to lunch unless accompanied by someone else.
- Sharing with them that physical contact between you two will never go past a hand-

shake or high five.

- Letting them know that you will not drive alone with them in a car.
- Telling them that you will do whatever you need to in order to show your appreciation without suggestions or comments on the physical side of things.

This is all part of planning to make decisions before emotions are involved.

Each of the 246 men cited in Dr. Hendrick's study believed it would never happen to them. But the Bible says, "Therefore let him who thinks he stands take heed that he does not fall." (1 Corinthians 10:12). The Bible also tells us, "Pride goes before a destruction..." (Proverbs 16:18a) So, to think that you are above a sexual fall is setting yourself up for failure. If we would just admit that we are men like other men and are in need of love, compassion, and physical contact, it will go a long way toward keeping us safe.

In Jerry White's book *Dangers Men Face*, he notes that he has seen some common threads and characteristics emerge from men who have fallen into sexual impurity. This is what he says underlies many men who have fallen morally;

- The macho image and a sense of dominance.
- A perceived failure in one's job or a blow to one's ego or pride.

- A feeling of being above the rules.
- Going easy on oneself in many areas like diet or exercise.
- Carelessly allowing oneself to be in places or situations that boost temptations.
- A roving and undisciplined eye.[14]

These are all characteristics which would cause ministers to be vulnerable to sexual temptation and sexual sin.

For multiple decades, Doctor Billy Graham has traveled the world sharing the gospel with countless audiences. He has also been a man who has been above scandal. When asked by a young man in ministry how he managed to stay out of the tabloids and to keep himself above reproach, Doctor Graham answered without hesitation, "Young man, I run scared. I run scared."

Millie Dienert has worked with the Billy Graham team for 40 years. She made this comment about working with the Billy Graham team, "I've always appreciated from a moral point of view how the men have been in their attitude toward the secretaries. The doors are always left open. There is a high regard for the lack of any kind of privacy where a boss and a secretary are involved. At times I thought they were going a little too far and that it wasn't necessary. But I'm glad they did it especially today. They have kept everything above reproach. When you are working on a long-term basis with the same person constantly in hotels where a wife is not present, that is a highly explosive situation. You have to take precautions. I have always respected the way they have handled things. It has been beautifully done."[15]

5 - EMBRACE THE DEPTH OF YOUR CALLING

Beyond counting the cost to someone else and yourself and realizing your vulnerability you also need to realize who you are. You're not just a man like any other man driven and lead about by your passions as so many dogs do. You're not just a man-you're a Christian man, a redeemed man, a forgiven man, and the son of the King. You've got to constantly act that way. As I mentioned earlier to agree to a call of God on your life and join with him in ministry is to agree that you are going to live your life in a fishbowl. People have a right to look at you a little differently. Others will be examining your life and there are not any rocks, underwater castles, or seaweed that you can hide behind escaping the eyes of those around you. That's not necessarily fair but, it is invariably true.

6 - BE VIGILANT DURING VICTORIES

Another area that you can use as a hedge against moral failure is to be careful of victory. Many times, men fall into sexual sin after something good has happened in their lives. This happened with King David. He had experienced great victories. The Kingdom was secure. His men were off to war and everything was going well. He stood up on his balcony and looked down and saw Bathsheba. You know how the rest of the story went. Tony Evans in his book *No More Excuses* sites that past success is no guarantee of future success. The fact that you haven't fallen in all those years has little to do with what might happen tomorrow.[16] Don't underestimate the power of passion. Passion is powerful. When you play with it you always want more. Don't live off of yesterday's spiritual victories. Keep your walk with God fresh every day.

So again, a man must be careful how he stands so that he does not fall. You must always realize that sin breeds consequences. Though the consequences may not be evident now, they will undoubtedly manifest themselves later on. They may not be problems for you, but they will be problems for someone along the way.

Not long ago, a very successful businessman was away on a trip. While out of town, he found himself in a situation that he didn't count on. It was late at night, and he was hungry. So, he went downstairs to the hotel restaurant and enjoyed a nice meal. He began to think about how great things were going and how quickly he was climbing the business ladder of success. At the same time, he began thinking about how disappointed he was with the physical side of his marriage. He wound up meeting a woman and had an affair with her. He completed his business in that city and returned to his family as if nothing had happened. But something had happened. Not only had he compromised his ideals and his vows. Not only had he had a sexual encounter outside of his marriage. He had been given more than just an evening of sexual pleasure. The woman had given him herpes. Unknowingly, he gave that disease to his wife and his wife became pregnant. Without knowing that she had the disease, she gave birth to a child who was born blind. The affair became public. His wife divorced him, and he no longer has contact with his children. He is now reaping what he has sown because sin carries with it consequences.

7 - IMMERSE YOURSELF IN GOD'S WORD AND PRAYER

The Bible says, "Thy word have I hid in my heart that I might not sin against thee." (Psalm 119:11). In understanding the advice that comes from God's word, a man can keep himself pure. As he sees the examples of those who have fallen it is easier for him to sidestep the land mines that come his way.

In Proverbs 7:6-27 Solomon talks to his son about a young man that he observed while looking through his window:

> *For at the window of my house I looked out through my lattice,*
> *⁷ And I saw among the naive, and*

discerned among the youths

A young man lacking sense,[8] passing through the street near her corner;

And he takes the way to her house, [9]in the twilight, in the evening,

In the middle of the night and in the darkness.[10] And behold, a woman comes to meet him, dressed as a harlot and cunning of heart.

[11] *She is boisterous and rebellious, her feet do not remain at home;*

[12] *She is now in the streets, now in the squares, and lurks by every corner.*

[13] *So she seizes him and kisses him and with a brazen face she says to him:*

[14] *"I was due to offer peace offerings; today I have paid my vows.*

[15] *"Therefore I have come out to meet you, to seek your presence earnestly, and I have found you.*

[16] *"I have spread my couch with coverings, with colored linens of Egypt.*

[17] *"I have sprinkled my bed with myrrh, aloes, and cinnamon.*

[18] *"Come, let us drink our fill of love until morning; let us delight ourselves with caresses.*

[19] *"For my husband is not at home, he has gone on a long journey;*

[20] *He has taken a bag of money with*

him, at the full moon he will come home."

21 With her many persuasions she entices him; with her flattering lips she seduces him.

22 Suddenly he follows her as an ox goes to the slaughter, Or as one in fetters to the discipline of a fool,

23 Until an arrow pierces through his liver; as a bird hastens to the snare,

So he does not know that it will cost him his life.

24 Now therefore, my sons, listen to me, and pay attention to the words of my mouth.

25 Do not let your heart turn aside to her ways, do not stray into her paths.

26 For many are the victims she has cast down, and numerous are all her slain.

27 Her house is the way to Sheol, descending to the chambers of death.

In examining that, Jerry White in his book *Dangers Men Face* states four things that should be in place to sidestep the problems this woman brings. If the young man Solomon observed had kept them in mind, perhaps she wouldn't have become a snare for him:

1. Don't let your desires get out of hand-control them.
2. Don't let yourself think about her-guard your mind.
3. Don't go near her-run from her tempting advances.
4. Guard your eyes. Filter the things you let yourself see-movies, photographs, or other women. "I made a covenant with my eyes not to look lustfully at a girl" (Job 31:3).[17]

If any man, and in particular a minister will adhere to these suggestions, ideas, and thoughts it will go a long way in keeping him pure; helping him to maintain the ministry that he has been called to do. If a man is wise, he will listen to the directives from Scripture, the advice from those who have fallen, and the aforementioned common-sense rules. Then when his ministry is over, he will be in a position to look back on his ministry life and be proud that he has run a clean race and hear the words we all long to hear, "Well done good and faithful servant."

SOURCE MATERIAL

[1]Steve Ferrar, Finishing Strong (Sisters, OR: Multnomah Press, 1995) p.64.

[2]Ibid. P.7.

[3]Harry W. Schaumburg, False Intimacy (Colorado Springs Co: Naupress 1997) p.189.

[4]H. Norman Wright, What Men Want (Ventura, CA.: Regal Books 1996) p.93.

[5]Jerry White, Dangers Men Face (Colorado Springs Co.: Naupress, 1997) p.81.

[6]Charles R. Swindoll, Growing Strong in the Seasons of Life (Portland OR.: Multnomah press 1983) p.94.

[7]Robert Hicks, The Masculine Journey (Colorado Springs Co.: Naupress 1993) pp.65-66.

[8]R. Kent Hughes, Disciplines of a Godly Man (Wheaton IL.: Crossway Books 1991) p.24.

[9]Farrar, pp.29-30.

[10]White, p.79.

[11]Charles R. Swindoll, The Finishing Touch (Dallas TX.: Word Publishing 1994) p.105.

[12]H.B. London, Surround Yourself, (Colorado Springs, Co.: Focus on the Family Magazine, June 1990).

[13]Rod Handley, Fellowship of Christian Athletes, 8701 Leeds Rd. Kansas City, Mo.   64129.

[14]White, pp. 29-30.

[15]Farrar, p.31.

[16]Tony Evans, No More Excuses, (Wheaton, IL. Crossway Books 1996) p.65.

[17]White, p.89.

ABOUT THE AUTHOR

Dr. Jirgal is a 1980 graduate of Gettysburg College where he became a four-time conference champion, All-American, and inductee to the Middle Atlantic Conference *All Century Team* in the pole vault. He holds an undergraduate degree in health education and physical education. Following graduation, he taught on the high school and college level while coaching football and track in both venues. He holds masters degrees in health education, sports medicine, and divinity, as well as a doctorate in ministry.

He has been the director of Sports Medicine at Wingate University, area director for the Fellowship of Christian Athletes and has served on the staff of Hickory Grove Baptist Church in Charlotte, N. C., as well as leading Lakeview Baptist Church, in Monroe, N. C. and Anderson Grove Baptist Church in Albemarle, N.C. He has served on the local board of directors for the Fellowship of Christian Athletes, the board of trustees at New Orleans Baptist Seminary and the ministerial board of Wingate University. He currently serves on the board of directors for The Carolina Study Center, and Fathers in Touch ministry.

Dr. Jirgal is the founder and director of *The Jirgal Leadership Institute* where he strives to equip people for success in leadership roles. He is the leadership pastor at Lee Park Church in Monroe, N.C. He and his wife Pam have three children, Joshua, Caleb, and Sarah. They reside in Mint Hill, N. C.

OTHER BOOKS BY DR. STEVEN JIRGAL

The Path of a Champion
Dirty Dozen
Dying to Live
Life Points
Principles of Wholeness
Mining the Mind of King Solomon
Intentional Steps
Encounters with the Christ
The Going to Bed Book
52 Words

**To learn more about the titles above,
visit www.JirgalLeadership.com.**

www.ingramcontent.com/pod-product-compliance
Lightning Source LLC
Chambersburg PA
CBHW060645030426
42337CB00018B/3450